STORY OF THE LOST TRAIL TO OREGON

This booklet, not in Howes, is No. 6710 in Smith, Pacific Northwest Americana, 1950 ed.

STORY
OF THE
LOST TRAIL
TO
OREGON

BY
EZRA MEEKER

YE GALLEON PRESS
FAIRFIELD, WASHINGTON
1998

Library of Congress Cataloging-in-Publication Data

Meeker, Ezra, 1830-1928.
    Story of the lost trail to Oregon.
    Reprint. Originally published: Seattle, Washington. : [s.n.], 1915.
  1. Oregon Trail. 2. Historical markers - Oregon Trail. 3. Overland
journeys to the Pacific. 4. Meeker, Ezra, 1830-1928. I. Title.
F880.M525   1984   979.5'041   84-5206

ISBN 0-87770-321-3 (pb.)

Reprinted in 1998

BIOGRAPHICAL DETAIL

Ezra Meeker, author of this booklet, was one of the grand old pioneers of Washington Territory. He was born in Butler County, Ohio, near Huntsville on December 29, 1830. His parents were Jacob Redding Meeker and Phoebe (Baker) Meeker. Seven years later the family moved to Covington, Indiana, and sometime later to a home near Indianapolis. Ezra Meeker had a few months of schooling, but this not being to his taste, he went to work at an early age operating the family farm while his father worked in a flour mill. At age twenty-plus, Ezra Meeker married Eliza Jane Sumner, this on May 13, 1851. In October of 1851 the young couple traveled to Iowa with an ox-drawn covered wagon. In the spring of 1852 the young couple, now with a baby, started out from Council Bluffs to join other emigrants traveling over the Oregon Trail. The party reached Portland on October 1, 1852. Next spring, with his wife, the baby and his brother, Oliver, they traveled north in search of a home in a new country. They settled on McNeil Island in Puget Sound, but giving this up, moved to the Puyallup Valley where Meeker built a log cabin. For more than half a century he remained in the valley farming, principally growing hops. In searching for a market for the hops, Meeker traveled to London where he spent several winters. He also made several trips to the Yukon region of Canada searching for gold.

Ezra Meeker wrote a number of books and booklets — Pacific Northwest and Oregon Trail history. Greatly interested in earlier emigration over the Oregon Trail, at age 75 he determined to travel again over the Oregon Trail in reverse direction, from Puyallup to eastern U.S. He began this journey on January 29, 1906, using the family covered wagon and ox team, marking various locations that he remembered from his 1852 journey. In 1910 he repeated this performance and in 1915 traveled by automobile over such portions of the Oregon Trail that he could reach. In 1924 at age ninety-three, followed part of the Oregon Trail route by airplane. In 1928, in his 98th year, he attempted again to travel from the Atlantic Coast back to Puyallup, but became ill and spent some time in a hospital in Detroit. He traveled to Seattle by train, but his days were numbered and two months later he died. In later years he attended many historical meetings where he was often photographed with white hair and beard, consequently a number of archival sources have original photographs. Despite his limited education and some carelessness in dating events, he was in his day rather widely known as an author. Despite much discouragement from a disinterested citizenry, he persisted in his efforts to have the Oregon Trail marked and publicized. The current revival of interest in the Oregon Trail is based in part on Meeker's efforts three-quarters of a century ago. It is perhaps unfortunate that Meeker's revision of his autobiographical writings on which he worked in his last years was never completed.

Story of the Lost Trail to Oregon

By EZRA MEEKER

Seattle, Washington.

Five Cents a Copy, Postpaid

February 20—1915—December 4

Washington State Building at the Panama-Pacific Exposition, February 20-December 4, 1915, San Franeisco, Cal.

THE EPIC of the "Oregon Trail," published by the New York *Evening Post* eight years ago, and herewith reproduced, is without a peer as a brief record of history.

This exposition edition of twenty thousand completes a series of reprints of one hundred and ten thousand copies.

The oxen mounted together with the prairie schooner wagon in which the trip was made across the continent, and to Washington city, now on exhibition in the Washington State Building, Panama Exposition, at San Francisco, will be transferred at the close of the exposition to Point Defiance Park, Tacoma, Wash., and housed in a large glass case for preservation.

Shown daily in moving pictures with lecture by Ezra Meeker in the Washington State Building at 11:30 A. M. and 3 P. M.

Fifty memorial granite monuments have been erected along the Oregon Trail. Now an earnest effort is being made to build a great national highway along the general route of the Trail as a memorial to the pioneers, to be known as PIONEER WAY.

The Lost Trail.

The search for the Oregon Trail has been prosecuted now for eight years and much of it recovered, and it is confidently expected all will be in the near future.

It is a wonderful story, that of the growth of the Oregon Trail. Why so many home builders with their families plunged into the then unknown wilderness across so wide a stretch of what was known as the "Great American Desert," no man can tell. Certain it is that no such record in the world's history can be found of so many people going so long a distance to found an empire, as they did, over the two thousand miles' stretch of the Oregon Trail. So long as this mystery or romance remains there will continue an abiding interest in this unsolved problem. Lovers hastened their union that they might share the danger and privation together across the unknown stretch; sedate heads of families as mysteriously were moved to risk all, that they might see the farther West; young men boldly moved out on the plains as if it were only a great "playground" where the sport of the chase would continue forever. It would seem that manifest destiny prompted the multitude, whatever may have ultimately governed their action. Three hundred thousand people traversed the Oregon Trail to beyond the summit of the Rocky Mountains and passed through that great rift in the mountains, the South Pass. Nature had

provided and pointed the way and in time we see un-
folded the final climax when the great wagon trains
began to roll through that wonderful break in the mountains, the South Pass of the Rocky Mountains.

Mystery surrounds the real discovery of the "Pass."
In prehistoric times the buffalo wore trails over the
summit. We know as little as to when the Indians followed. As already said, Nature had pointed the way.
The melting snows of mid-winter storms descending
from the higher levels formed the little river, Sweetwater, which in turn emptied into the North Platte,
and this in its turn formed its junction with the South
Branch and thence rolled placidly as a mighty river
to the greater Missouri. To follow the Oregon Trail
to within two miles of the summit of the South Pass
is to follow up the current of the waters described; the
route of the least resistance destined again to become
the Nation's highway, to the higher altitudes above
the clouds and almost up to the perpetual snow line,
7,450 feet above sea level.

Now we are over the summit and look out westward
over a vast plateau of high altitude a hundred miles
or more before we begin to descend into the Bear River
Valley, and down Bear River a short way and we are
near the Snake, which we follow, and finally to the
Columbia and the tide waters of the Pacific.

Lewis and Clark, in 1805, finally reached and de-
scended the Snake and Columbia, and that far were
on the general route of the Oregon Trail; then came
Hunt with his Astor party to traverse a part in 1811-12,
but the key, the South Pass, had not been discovered
yet, and not until ten years later a party of trappers
found and crossed over through the Pass. This was

in 1822 or 1823. Yet another ten years elapsed before any one person passed over the whole of the Oregon Trail. The glory of that achievement belongs to Nathn'l J. Wyeth, an intrepid Bostonian, who crossed with his wagons, following the wagon track already dimly worn a hundred miles west of the summit by other trappers and traders.

Wyeth built Ft. Hall in 1833, on the peninsula near the junction of the Port Neuff and Snake Rivers and advanced the wagon road that far. But formidable obstacles seemed to say "thus far and no farther" with a wagon road, and another ten years passes and "acres" of abandoned wagons covered the ground. Meanwhile Bonnyville had followed Wyeth to disaster; other traders appeared on the scene, and a war of efforts to secure the coveted furs continued. The missionaries had passed over. A few of the trappers had tired of their adventures and wore the Trail a little deeper on their way to the Columbia and to the tide waters of the Pacific. The home builders began to put in an appearance on the whole length of the Trail in the late '30's and early '40's, making the famous pathway a little deeper and wider—all failing, however, to carry their wagons farther than to Fort Hall and the Snake. Finally that great migration of 1843 of a thousand persons, men, women, and children, fixed the final route of the Trail by passing over it from end to end with their wagons and stock. No more heroic act is recorded in history than this of that great company opening their own wagon road from day to day for over six hundred miles west from Fort Hall. We now have the trail complete.

Word goes out there is a wagon road to the Pacific, and the eager throng each year wear the Trail deeper and deeper; the Mormons now appear with their ox wagons and carts, their hand carts and wheelbarrows, to deepen the Trail and line it with their dead—this in 1846-47. Then followed the California throng on the Oregon Trail for a thousand miles or more to stir the soil that the wind might carry it away, leaving the sunken pathway a little deeper. This in 1849. Now, again comes the throng—another high tide, to the Oregon country, when another ten years is tolled off and a great army cover the plains—gold seekers, home builders, religionists, and adventurers of every kind. Now we see the Trail filled with wagons two abreast, so numerous is the throng, and two trails appear for long stretches. The graves have become common; five thousand have died in the one year alone; what with the dead and dying, the panic that ensued, the intolerable dust, the parched lips and weakened frames, we may well wonder that the casualties were not greater. The Trail is now ten feet deep and a hundred wide in many places, but yet destined to be worn deeper and deeper by the return tide of stock in the fullness of time, a million a year for many years, trampling the graves into dust and wearing the Trail into almost incredible widths and depths—fifteen feet deep and two hundred feet wide in one place encountered tells the wonderful story better than song or fiction.

And yet long stretches were lost by the march of improvement; the farmer took no note of it in sentiment and plowed over it; city builders have erected brick blocks over where the Trail once ran, and so, what with great irrigation ditches destroying it with other like factors at work, small wonder we should call it the "Lost Trail."

But we are gradually recovering it from the oblivion in which it has slept. A stretch here and there is marked; the memories of past and passing generations have been revived, and finally with the help of the public land surveys of forty and fifty years ago, we are able to connect the whole so that we may say that for a continuous stretch of 1.600 miles we absolutely know where the Trail is, or was, with or without the visible marks upon the earth's surface.

To you who may read or hear these words, I conjure you to take heed and consider their importance. In the measure a generation views and studies the past the pace is set for the future. If we forget the deeds of our forebears, we discard the lessons of history and take a step backward in the march of civilization. In the measure a generation cherishes the past, so will it be for the future; for the love of country; for reverence of the flag; for the efforts of upbuilding the Nation. And, my friends, the recovering the Lost Trail has a deeper meaning than merely gratifying a whim or satisfying a feeling of curiosity.

See "The Oregon Trail." 150 pages, illustrated; paper cover; 30 cents post paid. Address Ezra Meeker, Seattle, Wash.

[From the *Ohio State Journal*, Tuesday Morning,
April 23, 1907.]

Tells the Story of Oregon Trail.

Ezra Meeker, Native Ohioan, Coast Pioneer, Outlines National Road Project.

His ox team and "prairie schooner" arouse much interest on the streets.

Ezra Meeker, a pioneer of the Oregon Trail, who is retraveling, in the ripeness of years, the trail he followed to the West in his youth, yesterday set forth to an audience on the streets of Columbus the object for which he is taking the long journey from Oregon to the capital of the Nation. The old man, with flowing white hair and beard, and his "prairie schooner" drawn by patient oxen, made a picturesque figure, surrounded by the stately evidences and busy life of modern civilization, as exemplified in a great city.

He did not lack hearers. His was not "the voice of one crying in the wilderness," but the voice of the wilderness and of the past calling in the city, with all its modernity, to its share to pay tribute to those who made modern American cities possible.

"Farmer" Meeker told the story of his life in words of simple earnestness and with no indirection. He is on his way to Washington, he said, to urge on the Government the building of an enduring monument to the builders of the West in the form of a great concrete thoroughfare which shall follow the Old National Road and the Oregon Trail from East to West.

"76 YEARS YOUNG."

He began by introducing himself as a citizen of Ohio, 76 years young. He said:

"My birthright entitles me to greet you as fellow-citizens. I was born in Huntsville, Butler County. This to me important event occurred December 29, 1830. Consequently many people persist in calling me old, while I insist that I am a little past 76 years young. However, I come among you as a stranger, having been reared near Indianapolis from early childhood, and from there, accompanied by my young wife, migrated to the old Oregon country in 1852. There I have since lived the simple life of a farmer with my chosen life partner, who still lives to greet me on my return to our home in the great State of Washington, of which we were a part when that portion of the old Oregon country became known as Washington Territory.

"Most of you wonder why a man at this time of life would cross the plain with an ox team at this age of the world and spend fifteen months in so doing when he could have come by rail all the way in five days, surrounded by all the comforts of life. I will tell you why. But first let me tell you about the team and outfit, as I know by the questions so oft repeated that this is uppermost in your mind. This off ox "Dave" came all the way from the stockyards at Tacoma and was an unbroken, wild Montana range steer. When I yoked him first he never before had had a rope on, except when branded. He is six years old, weighed when purchased 1,470 pounds, and now weighs 1,735, after having traveled on this trip over 2,800 miles from Puyallup, near Tacoma, to this city. Seventeen hundred miles out from my home the noble ox "Twist" died, from eating poisonous weeds, I think. Any way, he was in better working trim the forenoon he took sick than when the start was made, and was dead before sunset. To mate the ox left I purchased this fine steer on the near side, "Dandy," out of the stockyards at Omaha, and broke him in on the way. He, too, was a range steer that had never been handled. His weight when purchased was 1,470 pounds. He now tips the scales at 1,625 pounds.

"PRAIRIE SCHOONER.

"The wagon is of the type known as the 'Prairie Schooner,' that was in general use fifty years ago—wooden axle, necessitating the linchpin and tar bucket, with its swayback bed, which doubltess gave the name of this type of wagon, being, as you see, boat-shaped, suggestive of the name. And, my friends, the pioneers of the plains applied this likeness in a more literal sense than in a name only by utilizing them as boats in crossing rivers. I crossed the Great Snake River at two places with all of my belongings (except the cattle) with my wagon bed in 1852, and small wonder if I should look upon this type of the almost forgotten past akin to a feeling almost of reverence.

"One word as to that faithful companion, the Scotch collie dog 'Jim.' Jim has come all the way; has been a reliable watchman at night and cheerful companion of days—always good natured, except with the ox 'Dave.' They are mortal enemies.

"I will now tell you why this trip was made in this old-fashioned style. To perpetuate the identity of the old Oregon Trail, to honor the true heroes who made it, and to kindle in the breasts of the rising generation a flame of patriotic sentiment this expedition was undertaken. The ox team was chosen as a typical reminder of pioneer days, as an effective instrument to attract attention, arouse enthusiasm, and as a help to secure aid to forward the work; and I may say in passing that from the Missouri River to Puget Sound twenty-two monuments of enduring stone have been provided for by the people along the Trail, and most of them are now in place to stand guard for centuries, to the end that the memory of the old Trail shall not fall into oblivion and be forgotten by the generations to come.

"In one place (Baker City, Ore.) eight hundred school children contributed their mites to place a bronze tablet on the granite shaft erected by the citizens as a 'children's offering' to the memory of the pioneers. At Boise, Idaho, over one thousand children contributed sufficient to erect a granite shaft twelve feet high, which was placed on the statehouse grounds and dedicated in the presence of five thousand people. Again, at American Falls, Idaho, a cement shaft fourteen feet high, suitably inscribed, stands in the exact track of the Trail, within the confines of that growing city and in a park dedicated by a generous woman to protect a section of the Trail. It is known as 'Pioneer Park.'

"MEMORIAL JOURNEY.

"And so, along the route this journey came as an offering to gladden one's heart and to give us assurance that patriotism is not dead in the breasts of the people, though apparently it may be dormant, and that it but needs a spark, if I may be allowed the term, to keep alive the memories of the past.

"The ox team did it. I have seen old, gray-headed men stand almost by the hour and gaze at this outfit, seemingly oblivious of all other surroundings and with moistened eyes as the rush of old-time memories would irresistibly take possession of their minds. Do I not see some of them now? My friends of the later generations, take these thoughts to your hearts and see if you may not read a lesson.that will serve you well in after life.

"And who are these pioneers we wish to honor? And what particularly great achievement have we to record? you ask. Where is this old Oregon Trail? I will tell you.

"FIRM BRITISH RULE.

"In 1843 nearly a thousand men, women, and children crossed the Missouri River, traversed the Platte Valleys, crossed the Rocky Mountains through the South Pass, thence to and down Snake River to the Columbia, and to tidewater in the old Oregon country; the first wagon train that ever reached the Pacific Coast, and the first real migration of home builders to the Pacific Slope. Like a gathering storm of a summer day, these people had come together on the eastern border of the Indian country from widely scattered districts of the United States and pitched their tents near the buffalo herds on the western border of civilization. The Oregon question was unsettled, but hung in the balance. The Lynn bill granting 640 acres of land to each family, had passed the Senate. Whitman, the intrepid missionary, had returned overland the previous winter to save his mission, and preached Oregon in season and out of season. The Government was organizing an expedition under the leadership of Fremont to penetrate the dark country, of which so little was known.

"The British ruled Oregon, if not with an iron hand, certainly with firmness. The word of John McLaughlin, chief factor of the Hudson Bay Company, was the law of the land. He was known as the autocrat of the great Northwest. A mild-mannered man and, let it be said, a just man, aye more, a great man, yet he ruled under the auspices of the British Empire and was all the more dangerous to American interests and American rule because of his justness, which disarmed criticism while holding the country with a firm grip for the British Empire.

"Such were the conditions when this first wagon train of home builders arrived in Oregon. These intrepid men had built their own wagon road for full six hundred miles. They had overcome formidable obstacles in hewing their way. The widely advertised 'Pathfinder,' Fremont, had followed their trail instead of pointing the way. Whitman had traveled with them and encouraged them as guide, counselor, and physician, until duty led him to a sick bed at his mission. If they failed, starvation confronted them. Go ahead they must, for retreat was impossible. They were not in the position of the Pilgrims landing on Plymouth Rock, who could retreat to their ships. These people had, figuratively speaking, burned their bridges behind them. And yet a more formidable task lay in their path. They were intensely American in the highest sense that word implies. Go under the British rule they would not, and so, before the roofs were complete on the cabins of many of them, an American provisional government was formed, and what is more remarkable, in less than two years the British rule was ended and Oregon became independent American Territory, to become in after years the mother of American States instead of remaining, as these people found it, a British colony.

"HONOR THESE MEN.

"It is these pioneers as a class we are striving to honor, not particularly individuals. As I have said, twenty-two monuments line the way from Puget Sound to the Missouri River to bear witness to the achievements of the pioneers. But we are not content to rest here. We want a greater monument; a monument of utility that shall hand down to all succeeding generations the memory of the Old Trail and its pioneers, a national highway to be known as Pioneer Way, from the Missouri River to the Pacific; a way that shall make traffic practicable by the trackless car, a road of cement that shall be thronged with coming generations.

"I do not come among you soliciting financial aid, but I do ask your moral support, so that when this expedition reaches Washington and the proposition is laid before the President and Congress, they may know there is a public sentiment behind the movement."

Following the address a considerable amount of Mr. Meeker's literature was taken by the auditors. He will remain in the city all this week arousing interest in his project.

[From the New York *Evening Post,* Saturday, May 18, 1907.]

Last Blazes on the Oregon Trail.

Aged Pioneer Retraced His March of Fifty-four Years Before.

Ezra Meeker's journey from Puyallup to his Indiana home—many monuments erected along the way—famous travelers who trod the rough road's 2,000 miles—both the Oregon and Santa Fe trails now permanently marked.

Originally blazed for a portion of the way by De la Verendrye, in 1742; trodden a distance by Lewis and Clark as they pushed across the vast trans-Mississippi empire; worn by the trappers and adventurers of the first quarter of the nineteenth century, such men as Ezekiel Williams, General Ashley, "Jim" Bridger, Campbell, Fitzpatrick, Sublette, and Wilson Price Hunt, and made into a hard and smooth highway by the hardy Missourians rushing across the continent in search of gold, by the Mormons seeking a new land of liberty, and by countless soldiers of fortune, the famous Oregon Trail has at last been rescued from oblivion and marked with stone monuments, thanks largely to the work of one man, Ezra Meeker.

Starting from his home in Puyallup, Wash., on January 29, 1906, Mr. Meeker retraced his march of fifty-four years before, back along the Oregon Trail to its Eastern terminus on the Missouri River, then across

STORY OF THE LOST TRAIL TO OREGON

Iowa and Illinois to his Indiana home. As he journeyed, Mr. Meeker interested the people along the route in the importance of saving the Oregon Trail from oblivion. Their fathers and grandfathers had helped to make it, but the past was in a fair way to be forgotten. The line of a great transcontinental railroad parallels or covers the old Oregon Trail for much of its way to-day, but there were detours and stages to be marked before they were lost sight of entirely.

To this old trail, which was one of the great roadways of the Nation a century and a half century ago, has become known better than ever to the present generation. Between Puyallup and Omaha nineteen monuments have been erected. Ezra Meeker, after a year's travel, reached his Indiana home. His journey and his work ended. Not so the interest in the old trail, especially as it follows the marking of another old trail, the Santa Fé, through Kansas.

Before tracing the Oregon Trail across the country from the Missouri River to the Pacific Ocean and counting over those who wore it smooth, it might be well to summarize briefly Mr. Meeker's work in marking it.

INTERESTING THE PEOPLE.

After he left his Washington home, more than 2,500 people contributed to the erection of Oregon Trail monuments. At intervals along the route Mr. Meeker, with the aid of people for whom he and others blazed the way, erected monuments—a huge stone boulder here, a cairn of stones there, a signboard or post in another place. In Baker City, Oregon, the monument was erected by contributions received from eight hundred school children, all of whom were present when it was dedicated. At Boise, Idaho, Mr. Meeker camped for several days beside the postoffice. He spoke to the public school children of his object, and 1,200 contributed to purchase the granite monument which will mark the place where the old-timers passed through what is now a thriving city. The governor of the State and other State officers insisted that the monument be erected on the statehouse yard, and it was dedicated in the presence of more than three thousand people.

To erect a monument at the summit of South Pass, Mr. Meeker traveled eighty-four miles from a post-office, and twenty-four persons who reside in the neighborhood were the only witnesses of the event. The monument stands on the irrigation survey near Sweetwater, and is 7,450 feet above sea level, one of the highest of such landmarks in the country.

In many of the towns and places where monuments were erected, Mr. Meeker stayed to see the work done, but in many other instances he turned the matter over to a local committee appointed for that purpose.

BEGAN ON THE MISSOURI.

The Oregon Trail began, as did the Santa Fé Trail, leading to the Southwest, at the town of Independence, on the Missouri River. Practically, St. Louis was the eastern terminus, men and goods going up the Missouri River to Independence, and there taking wagon and setting out either for the Northwest or the Southwest.

The two trails were the same for forty-one miles, when, as the historian Chittenden remarks, a simple signboard was seen which carried the words, "Road to

Oregon." That signboard to-day, with its lack of ostentation and its epigrammatic clearness, would be worth more than its proverbial weight in gold to any State historical society.

There were branch trails that came into the road from Leavenworth and St. Joseph, striking it above the point of departure from the Santa Fé Trail; but the Oregon Trail proper swung off from this fork, running steadily to the northwest, part of the time along the Little Blue River, until at length it struck the valley of the Platte, so essential to its welfare. The distance from Independence to the Platte was 316 miles, the trail reaching the Platte about twenty miles below the head of Grand Island. The course thence lay up the Platte Valley to the two fords, about at the Forks of the Platte, 433 or 493 miles.

Here at the Forks was a point of departure in the old days. If one chose to follow the South Forks of the Platte he might bring up in the Bayou Salade, within reach of the Spanish settlements and the head of the Arkansas, or he might take the other arm and come out on the edge of the Continental Divide, much higher to the north.

The Oregon Trail followed the South Fork for a time, then swung over to the North Fork, at Ash Creek, 513 miles from Independence. It was 667 miles to Fort Laramie, which was the last post on the eastern side of the Rockies. Thence the trail struggled on up the Platte, keeping close as it might to the stream, till it reached the ford of the Platte, well up toward the mountains, and 794 miles out from Independence, nearly the same distance from that point as was the Santa Fé on the lower trail.

INDEPENDENCE ROCK.

A little farther on the trail forsook the Platte, 807 miles out from Missouri, and swung across to the valley of the Sweetwater. The famous Independence Rock, 838 miles from Independence, was one of the most noteworthy features along the trail. It marked the entrance into the Sweetwater district and was a sort of register, holding the rudely carved names of many of the hardy Western adventurers. By the Sweetwater the Oregon trailers were taken below the foot of the Bighorns, past the Devil's Gate, and up to that remarkable crossing of the Rockies known as South Pass, where Ezra Meeker dedicated his monument under such unusual circumstances, taking water from the irrigation ditches on the east side of the Continental Divide to irrigate the west side. This is 947 miles from the Missouri River.

Starting now down the Pacific side of the Great Divide, the traveler passed over 125 miles of somewhat forbidding country, crossing the Green River before he came to Fort Bridger, the first resting point west of the Rockies, 1,070 miles from the Missouri. This was a delightful spot in every way, and always welcomed by the Oregon trailers.

The Bear River was 1,136 miles from Independence, and to the Soda Springs, on the big bend of the Bear, was 1,206 miles. Thence one crossed over the height of land between the Bear and Port Neuf Rivers, the latter being Columbia water; and, at a distance of 1,288 miles from Independence, reached the very important point of Fort Hall, the post established by Nathaniel Wyeth. This was the first point at which the trail struck the Snake River, that great lower arm of the

Columbia, which came dropping from its source opposite the headwaters of the Missouri to point out the way to travelers.

At the Raft River was another point of great interest; for here turned aside the arm of the transcontinental trail that led to California. This fork of the road was 1,334 miles from the Missouri. Working as best it might from the Raft River, down the Great Snake Valley, touching and crossing and paralleling several different streams, the Oregon Trail proper ran until it reached the Grande Ronde Valley, at the eastern edge of the difficult Blue Mountains, 1,736 miles from the starting point. The railway to-day crosses the Blues exactly where the old trail did.

Then the route struck the Umatilla, and shortly thereafter the Columbia River. It was 1,934 miles to the Dalles, 1,977 to the Cascades, 2,020 miles to Fort Vancouver, and 2,134 to the mouth of the Columbia, though the trail proper terminated at Fort Vancouver.

Such was the Oregon Trail, traversed by hundreds and thousands of hardy adventurers, outlet of the Missouri rendezvousing station, a mighty highway across which surged the advance tide of a Nation's traffic.

BLAZERS OF THE TRAIL.

Who blazed and followed this historic highway, destined to be marked to posterity fifty years after its zenith? The Frenchman De la Verendrye was perhaps the first to tread a portion of the later Oregon Trail; since it is known that he forsook the Missouri River and started overland, possibly up the Platte, crossing some of the country which the Astorians saw later. This was in 1742. The trapper Ezekiel Williams, said to have been the first white man to cross the borders of what is now Wyoming, followed in the wake of Lewis and Clark, in 1807, and blazed a part of the way. Andrew Henry, whose name was given to a beautiful lake of the Rockies; Etienne Provost, the probable discoverer of historic South Pass; Campbell, Fitzpatrick, Sublette, Jim Bridger, General Ashley, Bonneville, and Walker—these are but a few of the leaders who blazed and trod the Oregon Trail, making it a well-defined highway before Fremont set out as a "pathfinder."

Then came Wilson Price Hunt, with his overland Astorians, seeking a way from the mid-Missouri to the Columbia River. Later, Robert Stuart and the returning Astorians were to mark out, east of the Continental Divide, the route of the trail for much of its length. Then came scores of trappers and traders; then Bonneville and his wagons, to deepen the trail, in 1832; and two years later, in 1834, Campbell and Sublette built old Fort Laramie on Laramie Creek, a branch of the Platte. Eight years later Fort Bridger was built by Jim Bridger, on a branch of the Green River.

In 1836 two women moved out into the West along the Oregon Trail. They were the wives of Whitman and Spalding, missionaries bound for Oregon. Father de Smet, a missionary also, followed in 1840; then more missionaries from New England, and two years later Frémont, as far, at least, as the South Pass.

So the Oregon Trail was blazed and tramped; traders, trappers, gold seekers, missionaries, colonists, until the highway stretched from the Missouri River to the Pacific Ocean. Years passed and railroads supplanted the old Oregon Trail; its very whereabouts was forgotten; disputes arose. Then an old man, almost eighty, with his grandchild, clambered into a prairie schooner, made in part of the one in which he had journeyed westward in 1852, and the Oregon Trail was retraced and marked with monuments, that a people and a Nation may not forget.—F. G. M.

[From the *Illinois State Register*, Sunday, November 6, 1910.]

The Lost Oregon Trail.

Ezra Meeker's Interesting Lecture Before the Y. M. C. A. Thursday Evening.

Telling of his adventures in his first trip across the continent while blazing the Oregon Trail, and then telling of his present journey, Ezra Meeker, the grizzled pioneer of Washington State, delivered a most interesting talk at the Y. M. C. A. on Thursday night.

He spoke as follows:

"THE LOST TRAIL

"I am to speak to-night of the lost trail of history, the 'Oregon Trail,' once so thronged with eager adventurous spirits, now a solitude in many intervening reaches, fading away from the memory of man and almost obliterated from the face of the earth.

"No more fascinating search can ever engage the mind of man than to follow the actual track of the Fathers that opened the way to conquer the land and wrest it from the native race and erect the standard of civilization in the wilderness and with the standard a barrier to an encroaching Nation whose grasp was tightening upon an empire—the Oregon country.

"Let me for a few moments follow the track as best we may of the throng of three-quarters of a century ago.

"We are on the left bank of that mighty, turbid river, the Missouri. All beyond to the westward is a blank. The Indians and the buffalo possess the land; we can not see that manifest destiny has set the seal upon the destruction of the one, though we may dimly realize the power of the other is destined to be broken in the march of civilization.

"The throng has crossed over; first by the adventurer in search of the golden harvest of furs, then the bold spirits of missionary fame, to be soon followed by the no less intrepid spirits, the home builders, who go out with all their belongings—their women and children, their cattle to cover a thousand hills, not forgetting nor neglecting to carry their trusty rifles, needed not only for defense, but for sustenance as well.

"THE OREGON TRAIL.

"The throng has disappeared. The generation that then toiled so diligently now sleep beneath the sod; a few only remain to tell the story of the great battle. Twenty thousand graves line the way of the great battlefield, or did, but alas! as like the track they made, have almost all fallen into oblivion. It is of this track, 'The Oregon Trail,' that I am to speak to-night. The converging columns that had crossed the river at various intervening points from Council Bluffs and the mouth of the Kaw River meet some two hundred miles out on the banks of the Platte, then a broad river of placid waters, wooded islands, and treacherous quicksands, but now a barren waste of shifting sand, for the water has gone to the land. We find traces of the track on either side of the river until the parting of the waters, known as the north and south forks. The way leads up the north fork. The track is worn deeper and wider, for all is concentrated here. The Oregon pioneers have broken the way; the Mormons have followed; then comes the gold hunter, the California exodus, all traveling the one track and jostling the home builders, still pressing onward for the fair land of Oregon.

"We are now on the Sweetwater; past Independence Rock, that great register of the passing throng; past the Devil's Gate, that rift in the mountain a hundred feet wide, with perpendicular walls nearly five hundred feet high, through which the water of the Sweetwater roars; past Split Rock, a chasm near by seemingly but a few feet wide and a thousand feet high; still on, up and up, crossing and re-crossing the little river, mounting higher and higher, finally leaving it for good and all. In less than three miles and with but a few hundred feet ascent we are above the mid-summer snow line and on the summit of the South Pass of the Rocky Mountains, 7,450 feet above sea level. Snow-capped, rugged mountains are in sight to the north and to the south ten or more miles; to the west, through the great break in the mountain known as South Pass, our track leads us on a high plateau for a hundred miles or more. The ancient highway is here in all its primitiveness and solitude, worn deep and wide into the flinty roadbed—twelve, twenty, seventy, ninety, aye two hundred feet wide and two, five, and fifteen feet deep. Remember, friends, I am giving you actual measurements—where the hoofs of stock and the grind of the wagon wheels had loosened the soil and the fierce winds had carried it away in impalpable dust or coarser sand, to stifle the breath of man or beast or smart the faces of the suffering pioneers.

"STRIKE SNAKE RIVER.

"But we must on; we are yet high up in altitude, five, six, and seven thousand feet for a hundred miles or more, until Bear River is reached; down Bear River a short way, past the sparkling soda springs—past that once famous but now silent Steamboat Springs, spouting at irregular intervals in the air; steadily on, bearing more to the north until we strike Snake River, then down the left bank past American Falls, Twin Falls, Shoshone Falls (well named the Niagara of the West), on down past the two Salmon Falls, upper and lower, and near by, where we follow the track of the decimated throng across the river to the north bank, over to and down Boise River, then back again across the Snake, soon to be left until its waters are encountered mingled with the waters of the Columbia. We are still on the trail that leads us up the Burnt River, the roughest piece of road yet encountered. On and on to the Grand Ronde Valley of pleasant memories, and up the seemingly impossible face of the Blue Mountain and into the welcome glades of the pine-covered forests, and then another stretch of dust and thirst to the broad Columbia, more than a mile wide, but suddenly lost in its grandeur of width and rushing in its greater grandeur of power through that chasm known as The Dalles, with a breadth of channel less than two hundred feet—a roaring torrent of unknown depth, a river turned on edge.

Near by and just below this wonderful gorge our visible track ends. The greater gorge through the Cascade Mountains obstructs the way, and here the all but famished pioneers took to the water, some in boats, some on rafts, some in their wagon-boxes, and floated down past the sunken forests, past most awe-inspiring scenery, to the Cascades, where we again for a short distance catch sight of the great trail around to the foot of the falls and to the tide waters of the great ocean beyond, beating back the almost resistless waters of the Columbia.

"THE BLAZERS OF THE TRAIL.

"Let me now turn our attention to the men and women who made this mighty highway, the longest continued track in the world, and let me say in passing, the trail of the greatest tragedies, not forgetting that trail of sorrow that leads to Siberia.

' The pioneers of that day were stalwarts—stalwarts in strength, in courage, in integrity, in manly and womanly virtue. They were nearly all frontiersmen, as well trained to the rifle as with the plow. Their habits of life were simple; clad, many of them, in homespun, with shoes made of cowhide on the cobbler's bench in the home, hats patched in ways indescribable, small wonder if they did present an uncouth appearance. But under all this a native wit prevailed, and if not schooled in Greek or Latin literature, they had learned their lessons well in the greatest school of all—life experience of industry, frugality, and for lack of a better name, one may call homely virtues.

"As the throng moves out into the Indian country, (I now have in mind the movement in which I took a part), there soon developed weak points in the preparation for so great a trip, as well as weak bodies as compared with the stronger. Useless plunder soon began to make its appearance in abandoned piles along the roadside; but little later great piles of flour, bacon, sugar, in fact all sorts of provisions, were abandoned, to relieve the overloaded wagons and overburdened teams. This began even before that dreadful scourge of cholera struck our columns. The throng was so great that all could not get into one track, and to this day traces of these parallel trails are to be found. There seemed at first some sort of orderly organization of companies like that of military rule, which, however, it was soon found were held together as like with a rope of sand. When the panic came, one might say that all organization ceased. The struggle for mastery of the road night and day began. The scene may well be likened to the retreat of a defeated and discouraged army pressed by a victorious foe. Small wonder if friends parted and enemies came together in the face of a common danger. I camped four days with a stricken brother to see sixteen hundred wagons pass. The loss of life was appalling. I have oftentimes refrained from telling the dreadful story, knowing full well that many would believe it incredible.

"Fully five thousand persons laid down their lives in that one year alone (1852), for the scourge followed us for over a thousand miles and lined the trail with fresh-made graves, one might almost say from one end to the other. While this was the chief cause of the great loss of life, there were others contributing, such as the lack of proper food, the irregular supply and impurity of water, the stifling dust, the anxiety to wear upon the iron will of the strongest. Enough has been said to justify me to say that the Oregon pioneers fought a veritable battle in their march to the Oregon country and that the 'Oregon Trail' became a great battlefield of history. This recital, my friends, remember covers but one year, while the growth and use of the trail covers a period of twenty-five years, in which it is estimated fully 300,000 people passed over it and, as I have said, twenty thousand died on the way.

"PRESERVATION OF TRAIL.

"Small wonder that with such an experience and with such memories the generation that has now so nearly passed over to the 'Greater Trail' should yearn to see their track preserved and their history recorded. We know by the records that forty years ago this thought took possession of many minds. We know that it was not from a morbid craving for notoriety, but from a sincere desire that an important chapter in history should be written. The conquering of the farther West, written in the blood of many martyrs, is a theme not only to fire the imagination, but likewise to bring a second sober thought for the duties of the hour, to preserve the legacy handed down to the present generation, to impel the study of the old-time ways, to compare the present with the past, remembering that all changes are not betterments. To preserve the history of a Nation is to perpetuate its existence and build up its righteousness. To teach a lesson of the virtues of the generation that have passed brings to the forefront their shortcomings as well, thereby impelling the younger generation to practice the one and avoid the other. And so with these thoughts in mind, this work to recover the 'Lost Trail' has been undertaken and the efforts made to arouse the Nation to complete the work.

"On the 29th of January, 1906, I left my home in Puyallup, Wash., with one ox and one unbroken steer and this old=time wagon now in your city, built from the remains of three old wagons that had crossed over with the throng of 1852-53, and drove out in search of the trail and made an attempt to preserve its identity with granite markers. The people turned out almost en masse, but would not contribute to a general fund, but would lend a willing hand to erect memorial monuments in centers of population. I can only give you a very brief account of that trip. My fortune and misfortunes for the nine months required to retrace as best we could the old trail makes quite a story, but I can only here briefly, very briefly, tell it. We could find traces of it here and there, and then lose it. Part had been fenced up, the fields plowed, and all visible signs gone. In other places nature had been at work. The storms of a half century have changed the face of the country, the river crossings and other landmarks, by growth of vegetation and otherwise. Then again, cities have been built over it, great irrigation ditches have been dug, and so it became evident it would be impossible to recover the whole of the old track without more ample means. On that trip, however, twenty-two granite monuments give evidence of the interest taken, for the people paid for them as I passed along; but when the Missouri River was crossed and a halt made to take account of stock, I then more fully realized the work had failed. To be sure, we had succeeded in getting up twenty-two monuments, but what was twenty-two monuments for a trail twenty-two hundred miles long? A monument for every hundred miles. On the way many boulders had been marked, wooden posts set—but the expedition as planned had failed. But financial success had come from an unexpected sale of my little book.

"A NATIONAL WORK.

"A resolution was formed to go on to Washington, D. C., to ask Congress to make it a national work, and so in twenty-two months to a day from leaving my home I drove on to the White House grounds, received instant recognition from the hands of President Roosevelt, followed by the introduction of a bill appropriating fifty thousand dollars to complete the work. I can not tarry to tell you of the varied fortunes that beset that measure farther than to say that it is now pending in both Houses of Congress and has been favorably reported by the Committee of the House and amended, requiring an accurate estimate of the cost to complete the work before any of the appropriation should become available.

"And so a second trip over the Trail became necessary to ascertain the number of monuments required, estimate their cost, and report the findings to the Congress. And that is what I have been doing this season just passed. I left my home the 12th of March and again have driven over and along near by the Trail and have actually recovered sixteen hundred miles of the old track."

"And Joshua said unto them, 'Pass over before the ark of the Lord your God in the midst of Jordan and take you every man of you a stone upon his shoulder according unto the number of the tribes of the children of Israel. That this may be a sign among you *that* when your children ask *their fathers* in time to come, saying, what *mean* you by these stones;

" 'Then ye shall answer them, That the water of Jordan were cut off before the ark of the covenant of the Lord when it passed over Jordan; and these stones shall be for a memorial unto the children of Israel forever.' "

"So say we now take every man of you a stone to cast upon the monument of the Oregon Trail as hallowed ground trod by the men who opened the way for this grand civilization, that their fame shall abide with us and their very tracks shall be preserved as a sign among you that when your children ask *their* fathers in time to come saying what mean ye by these stones then ye shall answer them, these stones shall be for a memorial unto the pioneers who gave their lives that we might possess this heritage."

STORY OF THE LOST TRAIL TO OREGON

]From the "History of the Fur Trade of the Far West,"
by Hiram Martin Chittenden; published by
Francis P. Harper, New York.]

"This wonderful highway was in its broadest sense a national road, although not surveyed or built under the auspices of the Government. It was the route of a national movement—the migration of a people seeking to avail itself of opportunities which have come but rarely in the history of the world, and which will never come again. It was a route, every mile of which has been the scene of hardship and suffering, yet of high purpose and stern determination. Only on the steppes of Siberia can so long a highway be found over which traffic has moved by a continuous journey from one end to the other. Even in Siberia there are occasional settlements along the route, but on the Oregon Trail in 1843 the traveler saw no evidence of civilized habitation except four trading posts, between Independence and Fort Vancouver.

"As a highway of travel the Oregon Trail is the most remarkable known to history. Considering the fact that it originated with the spontaneous use of travelers; that no transit ever located a foot of it; that no level established its grade; that no engineer sought out the fords or built any bridges or surveyed the mountain passes; that there was no grading to speak of nor any attempt at metalling the roadbed, and the general good quality of this two thousand miles of highway will seem most extraordinary."

After describing the general good quality of the Trail in the early days, Mr. Chittenden continues his narrative: "But not so when the prairies became dry and parched, the road filled with stifling dust, the stream beds mere dry ravines, or carrying only alkaline water, which could not be used; the game all gone to more hospitable sections, and the summer sun pouring down its heat with torrid intensity. It was then the Trail became a highway of desolation, strewn with abandoned property, the skeletons of horses, mules, and oxen, and, alas! too often, with freshly-made mounds and head-boards that told the pitiful tale of suffering too great to be endured. If the Trail was the scene of romance, adventure, pleasure, and excitement, so it was marked in every mile of its course by human misery, tragedy, and death."

READERS of this booklet are invited to examine my "Oregon Trail," recently issued at the nominal cost of 30 cents, giving an account of my trip across the plains with an ox team during the year 1852, and also of the more recent drive across the continent and to Washington city, together with an autobiography; 150 pages; paper; 30 cents post paid.

"Pioneer Reminiscences, the Tragedy of Leschi," 550 pages; elegant silk cloth binding; post paid, $3.00.

Twenty-five short pioneer stories for children; 30 cents, post paid.

Twenty-five post card views with story on card—an illustrated history of the drive across the continent with the ox team; 25 cents, post paid.

Address
EZRA MEEKER,
WASHINGTON STATE BUILDING,
Panama-Pacific Exposition, San Francisco, or Seattle, Wash.

BIBLIOGRAPHY OF WORKS BY EZRA MEEKER

Washington Territory West of the Cascade Mountains. Olympia, Printed at the Transcript Office, 1870. 52 p.
Reprinted 1921 as chapter 6 of *Seventy Years of Progress in Washington.*

Hop Culture in the United States. Puyallup, Washington Territory, 1883. 170 p.

Catalog of Exhibits of Washington Territory at the American Exposition, New Orleans, Nov. 10, 1885 to April 1, 1885. New Orleans, W.B. Stanbury & Co. 1886. 32 p.

Local History. Address delivered before the Pierce County Teachers Institute. Tacoma, 1903. 13 p.

Who Named Tacoma? Address to the Washington Historical Society, Tacoma, Jan. 22, 1904.

Annual Address of Ezra Meeker, President of the Washington Historical Society. Tacoma, Washington, n.d. Contains the address published elsewhere under the title *Who Named Tacoma?* 1904.

Pioneer Reminiscences of Puget Sound; the Tragedy of Leschi . . . . Seattle, Washington, Lowman & Hanford, 1905. 554 p.

The Ox Team; or, The Old Oregon Trail, 1852-1906. Indianapolis, 1906. 248 p. reprinted Omaha, 1906, and New York, 1907.

Ventures and Adventures of Ezra Meeker . . . . Seattle, 1908. 384 p. reprinted Seattle, 1909, Rainier Printing Co. Later ed., Seattle, 1916, published under title *The Busy Life of Eighty-Five Years of Ezra Meeker.*

Personal Experiences on the Oregon Trail Sixty Years Ago. Seattle, 1912. 150 p. First published under the title *The Ox Team; or The Old Oregon Trail, 1852-1906.*

Story of the Lost Trail to Oregon. Seattle, 1915. 32 p. reprinted 1921.

Ezra Meeker's Pioneer Short Stories For Children. San Francisco, 1915. 97 p.

Ezra Meeker's Short Stories for Children. Tacoma, n.d. 100 p.

The Busy Life of Eighty-Five Years. Seattle, 1916. 399 p. Originally published as *Ventures and Adventures of Ezra Meeker.* 1908, 1909.

George Bush; review of J.E. Ayer: *George Bush, the Voyageur.* n.d., n.p. (1916?)

Seventy Years of Progress in Washington . . . . Seattle, 1921. Includes facsimile reproduction of *Washington Territory Westof the Cascade Mountains,* Olympia, 1870.

Ox-Team Days on the Oregon Trail. Yonkers-on-Hudson, 225 p. 1922, 1923,
  1925, 1932.
  Reprinted World Book Co., 1927. See entry above for 1906 and 1907.

Old and Historic Fort Hall. New York, 1925.

Kate Mulhall, a Romance of the Oregon Trail. New York, 287 p. (1926).

Covered Wagon Centennial and Ox Team Days. World Book Co., 1932.

The Ezra Meeker titles usually were printed in fair-sized editions and none are
considered rare. It is obvious that Meeker had considerable success as an author to
an uncritical public. He is little read today, but any of the Meeker titles are
considered collectable by collectors of PNW material. Kate Mulhall was his only
novel. His work falls into the category of recollections and ideas of the old timer,
and one who enjoyed the role.

COLOPHON

The Ezra Meeker, *THE STORY OF THE LOST TRAIL TO OREGON* is from the workshop of Glen Adams, which is located in the sleepy country village of Fairfield, southern Spokane County and one township removed from the Idaho line. Fairfield is located on Highway 27 which runs from Opportunity to Tekoa. The text is a facsimile of the 1915 edition with added biographical material. Additional typesetting for this edition and design work was done by Teresa Ruggles. Photography and film stripping was done by Dustin Newlun, who also burned the printing plates. Trevor Del Medico did the printing using a Heidelberg, model KORS. Folding was done by Garry Adams using a 26x40 Baum Dial-O-Matic folding machine. Paper binding was also completed by Garry Adams using a Mark II Sulby binding machine. This was a fun project. We had no special difficulty with the work.